Ex-Library: Friends of
Lake County Public Library

W9-AMC-070

"I Have a Song to Sing, O!"

AN INTRODUCTION TO THE SONGS OF GILBERT AND SULLIVAN

Selected and edited by **JOHN LANGSTAFF**

Illustrated by **EMMA CHICHESTER CLARK**

Piano arrangements by **BRIAN HOLMES**

MARGARET K. McELDERRY BOOKS
New York
Maxwell Macmillan Canada
Toronto
Maxwell Macmillan International
New York • Oxford • Singapore • Sydney

LAKE COUNTY PUBLIC LIBRARY

3 3113 01387 5119

Text copyright © 1994 by John Langstaff
Illustrations copyright © 1994 by Emma Chichester Clark
Piano arrangements copyright © 1994 by Brian Holmes
All rights reserved. No part of this book may be reproduced or transmitted in any form or
by any means, electronic or mechanical, including photocopying, recording, or by any
information storage and retrieval system, without permission in writing from the Publisher.

Margaret K. McElderry Books
Macmillan Publishing Company
866 Third Avenue, New York, NY 10022

Maxwell Macmillan Canada, Inc.
1200 Eglinton Avenue East, Suite 200, Don Mills, Ontario M3C 3N1

Macmillan Publishing Company is part of
the Maxwell Communication Group of Companies.

First edition
Printed in Hong Kong on recycled paper
The text of this book is set in Palatino.
The illustrations are rendered in watercolor.
10 9 8 7 6 5 4 3 2 1

Library of Congress Cataloging-in-Publication Data
Sullivan, Arthur, Sir, 1842–1900.
    [Operas.   Vocal scores.   Selections]
    I have a song to sing, O! : an introduction to the songs of Gilbert and Sullivan / selected and
edited by John Langstaff ; illustrated by Emma Chichester Clark ; piano arrangements by Brian
Holmes. — 1st ed.
    1 score.   Includes chord symbols.
    Summary: An illustrated collection of songs from famous operettas by Gilbert and Sullivan.
    ISBN 0-689-50591-4
    1. Operas—Excerpts—Juvenile—Vocal scores with piano. [1. Songs. 2. Operas—
Excerpts.]   I. Gilbert, W. S. (William Schwenck), 1836–1911. II. Langstaff, John M.
III. Chichester Clark, Emma, ill. IV. Holmes, Brian, date. V. Title.
M1507.S95L3   1994   93-10215

For my young friends . . .

Singing Gilbert and Sullivan at home with family and friends can be great fun. When I was growing up with my brother and sister, our parents sang with us and told us the stories of the operettas. They described the stage characters, and then we would try to *act out* some of the parts as we sang the songs. There were solos, duets, and trios we performed together, with everyone joining in the rousing chorus refrains.

The plots of the operettas are quite splendidly absurd, and that adds to the overall humor. The words of individual songs can be very amusing. (You may have to ask what some of the old-fashioned words mean!) Go and see stage productions when you can. You'll be surprised at how quickly you'll pick up and remember the catchy tunes and words, and the way the characters act—and even dance—while they sing. Make up your own actions as you sing these songs at home or in school. Emma Chichester Clark's delightful pictures will give you a good idea of the characters and how playful they can be. Reading the stories of these operettas, which may be found in collections of Gilbert and Sullivan in the public library, is a good way to discover the plots and how the songs fit in. But you don't need to know the stories in order to enjoy singing these tuneful songs.

For this collection, I've chosen songs that I think will be particularly fun for you to sing. As you are introduced to these songs and sing them, you'll find that you will want to learn lots *more* Gilbert and Sullivan.

—JOHN LANGSTAFF

P. S.   We've added guitar chords for most of these songs, should you want to try singing them with guitar accompaniment rather than with piano. Capo positions are also suggested for those chords that may be difficult.

To Ken, David, and Esther
—remembering our singing
together around the piano with
Mother and Dad
  —J. L.

For Finn and Will
  —E. C. C.

To Jerry, J. F., and Jolynda
  —B. H.

Contents

We Sail the Ocean Blue

from H.M.S. PINAFORE

Bright and bouncy (♩ = 96)

We sail the o-cean blue, And our sauc-y ship's a beau-ty; We're so-ber men and true, And at-ten-tive to our du-ty. When the balls whis-tle free O'er the bright blue sea, We stand to our guns all day. When at an-chor we ride On the Ports-mouth tide, We've

1

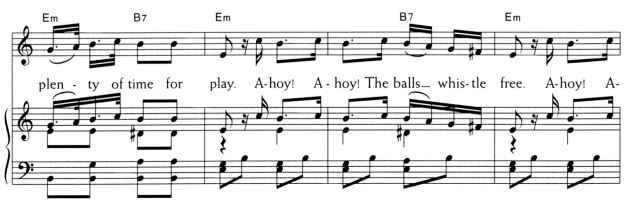

plen - ty of time for play. A-hoy! A-hoy! The balls— whis-tle free. A-hoy! A-

hoy! O'er the bright— blue— sea, We stand to our guns, to our guns all

day._____ We— sail the o-cean blue, And our sauc-y ship's a

beau - ty; We're— so-ber men and true, And at - ten-tive to our

duty. Our sauc-y ship's a beau-ty, We're at-ten-tive to our

du-ty; We're so-ber men and true, We sail the o - - - - cean

blue.

rit.

I Am the Monarch of the Sea

from H.M.S. PINAFORE

With matter of fact haughtiness (♩ = 144)

I am the mon-arch of the sea, The rul-er of the Queen's Na-

vee, Whose praise Great Brit-ain loud-ly chants, And we are his sis-ters and his

cou-sins and his aunts, His sis-ters and his cou-sins and his aunts! When at

an-chor here I ride, My bo-som swells with pride, And I

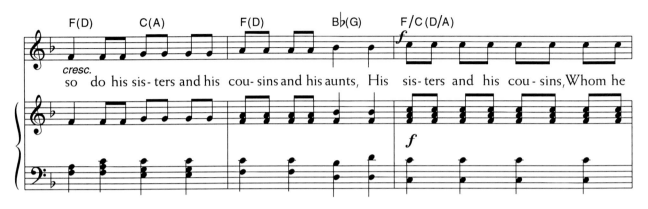

so do his sis-ters and his cou-sins and his aunts, His sis-ters and his cou-sins, Whom he

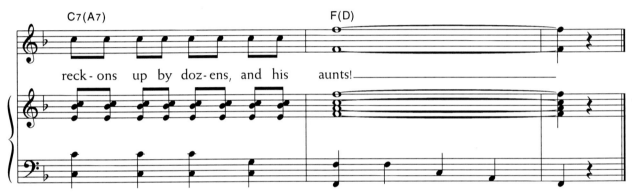

reck-ons up by doz-ens, and his aunts!_____

I'm Called Little Buttercup

from H.M.S. PINAFORE

Lilting ($\dot{\text{o}}$ = 48)

Little Buttercup

I'm called lit-tle But-ter-cup, dear lit-tle But-ter-cup, Though I could

Pedal freely

nev-er tell why, But still I'm called But-ter-cup, poor lit-tle

But-ter-cup, Sweet lit-tle But-ter-cup I! I've snuff and to-

bac-cy and ex-cel-lent jack-y, I've scis-sors and watch-es and knives;

I've rib-bons and la-ces to set off the fa-ces Of pret-ty young sweet-hearts and wives. I've trea-cle and tof-fee, I've tea and I've cof-fee, Soft tom-my and suc-cu-lent chops; I've chick-ens and con-ies and pret-ty po-lo-nies, And ex-cel-lent pep-per-mint drops.

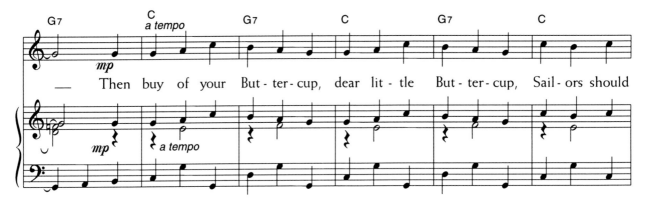

Then buy of your But-ter-cup, dear lit-tle But-ter-cup, Sail-ors should

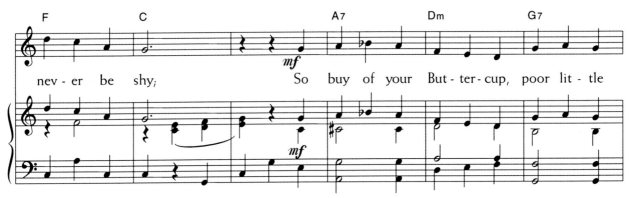

nev-er be shy; So buy of your But-ter-cup, poor lit-tle

But-ter-cup, Come! Of your But-ter-cup, buy!

I Am the Captain of the Pinafore

from H.M.S. PINAFORE

Jaunty and boastful (♩ = 96)

la-ted to a peer, I can hand, reef, and steer, Or ship a sel-va-

gee; I am nev-er known to quail At the fu-ry of a gale, And I'm

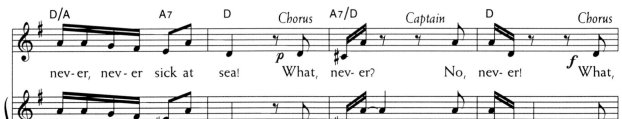

nev-er, nev-er sick at sea! What, nev-er? No, nev-er! What,

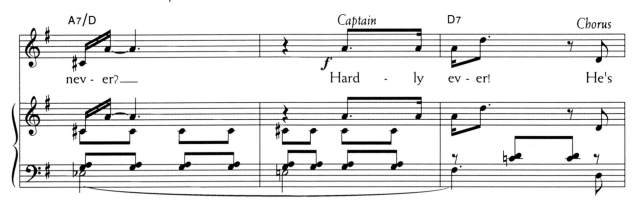

nev-er?___ Hard-ly ev-er! He's

hard-ly ev - er sick at sea! Then give three cheers and

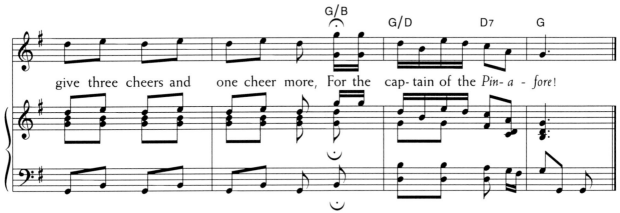

one cheer more, For the har - dy cap-tain of the *Pin - a - fore!* Then

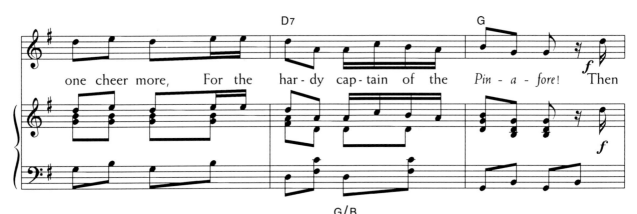

give three cheers and one cheer more, For the cap-tain of the *Pin - a - fore!*

When I Was a Lad

from H.M.S. PINAFORE

*Capo III

polished up the handle of the big front door. I
copied all the letters in a big, round hand. I
pass examination at the institute. That

Sir Joseph

polish'd up that handle so carefullee That
copied all the letters in a hand so free That
pass examination did so well for me That

polished up that handle so carefullee That
copied all the letters in a hand so free That
pass examination did so well for he That

now I am the ruler of the Queen's Navee. He
now I am the ruler of the Queen's Navee. He
now I am the ruler of the Queen's Navee. That

Chorus

now he is the rul-er of the Queen's Na - vee.
now he is the rul-er of the Queen's Na - vee.
now he is the rul-er of the Queen's Na - vee.

Sir Joseph

4. Of le - gal know-ledge I ac - quired such a grip That they
5. I grew so rich that I was sent By a
6. Now, lands-men all, who - ev - er you may be, If you

took me in - to the part - ner - ship, And that
pock - et bor - ough in - to Par - lia - ment. I
want to rise to the top of the tree, If your

ju - nior part - ner - ship, I ween, Was the
al - ways vot - ed at my par - ty's call, And I
soul is - n't fet - tered to an of - fice stool, Be

that kind of ship so suit - ed he That
thought so lit - tle they re - ward - ed he By
close to your desks and nev - er go to sea, And you

Eb(C)   F7(D7)   Bb(G)

now he is the rul - er of the Queen's Na - vee.
mak - ing him the rul - er of the Queen's Na - vee.
all___ may be rul - ers of the Queen's Na - vee.

I Have a Song to Sing, O!

from THE YEOMEN OF THE GUARD

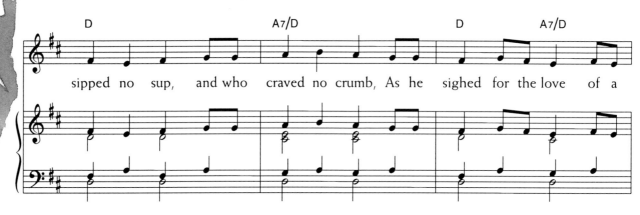

sipped no sup, and who craved no crumb, As he sighed for the love of a

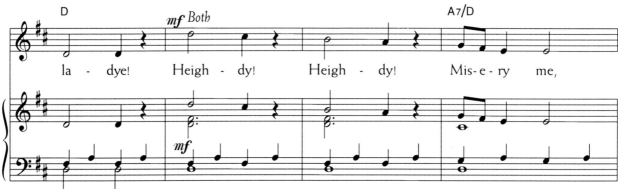

la - dye! Heigh - dy! Heigh - dy! Mis-e-ry me,

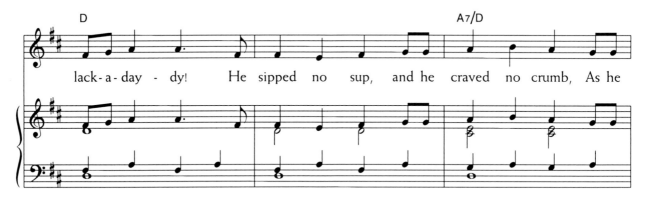

lack-a-day - dy! He sipped no sup, and he craved no crumb, As he

sighed for the love of a la - dye!

2nd verse

Elsie

I have a song to

sempre sostenuto

sing, O! What is your song, O?_____

Jack Point

D

Elsie

It is sung with the ring Of the songs maids— sing Who love with a love life-

A7/D   D

long, O! It's the song of a mer-ry maid, peer-ly proud, Who

A7/D   D   A7/D

loved a lord, and who laughed a-loud At the moan of a mer-ry-man,

D   A7/D   D

mop - ing mum, Whose soul was sad, and whose glance was glum, Who

sipped no sup, and who craved no crumb, As he sighed for the love of a

la - dye! Heigh - dy! Heigh - dy! Mis - e - ry me,

lack - a - day - dy! He sipped no sup, and he crav'd no crumb, As he

song of a pop-in-jay, brave-ly born, Who turned up his no - ble
pea - cock pop-in-jay, brave-ly born, Who turned up his no - ble

nose with scorn At the hum - ble mer - ry maid, peer - ly proud, Who
nose with scorn At the hum - ble heart that he did not prize; So she

loved a lord, and who laughed a - loud At the moan of the mer-ry-man,
begged on her knees— with down-cast eyes for the love of the mer-ry-man

mop - ing mum, Whose soul was sad and whose glance was glum, Who
mop - ing mum, Whose soul was sad and whose glance was glum, Who

sipped no sup, and who craved no crumb, As he sighed for the love of a
sipped no sup, and who craved no crumb, As he sighed for the love of a

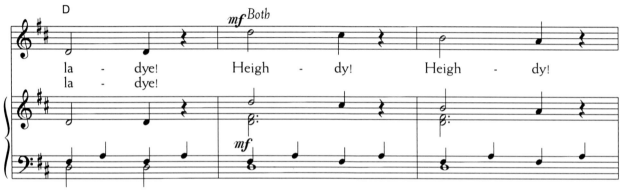

la - dye! Heigh - dy! Heigh - dy!
la - dye!

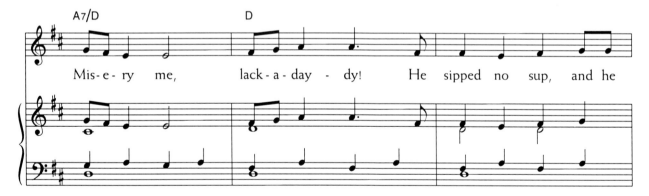

Mis-e - ry me, lack-a-day - dy! He sipped no sup, and he

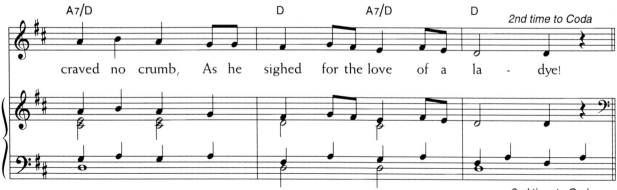

craved no crumb, As he sighed for the love of a la - dye!

2nd time to Coda

31

Coda

Heigh - dy! Heigh - dy! Mis - e - ry me, lack - a - day - dy! His

Coda

pains were o'er, and he sighed no more, For he lived in the love of a

la - dye!

A Wand'ring Minstrel, I

from THE MIKADO

Lilting (♩· = 72)

Nanki-Poo

A wan - d'ring min - strel I,   A thing of
shreds_____ and patch - es,   Of bal - lads, songs, and snatch - es,   And
dream - y lul - la - by!_____   My ca - ta - logue is long, Thro' ev - 'ry
pas - sion rang - ing,   And to your hu - mours chang - ing   I

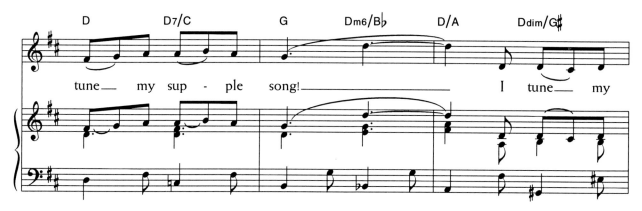

tune___ my sup - ple song!_____ I tune___ my

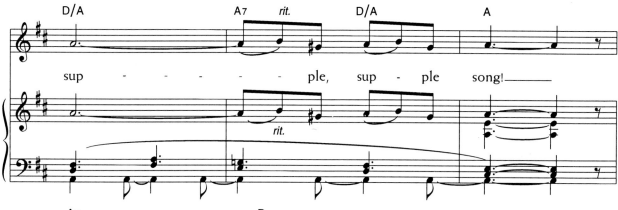

sup - - - - ple, sup - ple song!_____

Lul - - la - by!

36

Titwillow

from THE MIKADO

Quiet and sad (♩. = 60)

On a tree by a riv-er a lit-tle tom-tit Sang___ "Wil-low, tit-wil-low, tit - wil-low!"___ And I said to him, "Dick-y-bird, why do you sit Sing-ing 'Wil-low, tit-wil-low, tit -

Three Little Maids from School

f r o m THE MIKADO

Flirtatious (♩ = 104)

Trio

Three lit-tle maids from school are we, Pert as a school-girl well can be, Filled to the brim with girl-ish glee,___

Yum-Yum

Three lit-tle maids from school! Ev'-ry-thing is a source of___ fun.

Peep-Bo

No-bod-y's safe, for we care for___ none!

41

Three lit-tle maids from school! *f* Three lit-tle maids_____ from

school!

Fine

Yum-Yum

One lit-tle maid is a bride, Yum - Yum,

Peep-Bo

Two lit-tle maids in at - ten-dance come,

Pitti-Sing

Three lit-tle maids is the to-tal sum,

Trio

Three lit-tle maids from school!

43

Yum-Yum

From three lit-tle maids take one a-way,

Peep-Bo

Two lit-tle maids re - main, and they

Pitti-Sing

Won't have to wait ver-y long, they say,

Trio

Three lit-tle maids from school!

D.S. al Fine

D.S. al Fine

The Flowers That Bloom in the Spring

from THE MIKADO

Light and dancelike (♩. = 80)

The flow-ers that bloom in the spring, Tra-la, Breathe prom-ise of mer-ry sun-shine, As we mer-ri-ly dance and we sing, Tra-la, We wel-come the hope that they bring, Tra-la, Of a sum-mer of ro-ses and wine, Of a sum-mer of ro-ses and

Capo III

45

wine; And that's what we mean when we say that a thing Is

wel-come as flow-ers that bloom in the spring. Tra - la - la-la-la,___ Tra -

la - la-la - la,___ The flow -ers that bloom in the spring. Tra -

la - la-la - la,___ Tra - la - la-la - la,___ Tra - la-la-la - la - la!

When the Night Wind Howls

from RUDDIGORE

skies. / men,

When the foot - pads quail / And a - way they go,

at the night bird's wail, / with a mop and a mow,

and / to the

black dogs / rev - el

bay / that

at the moon, / ends too soon,

Then is the spec - tres' / For cock crow lim - its our

hol - i - day, / hol - i - day,

the

then is the ghosts' / dead of the night's

high / high

noon. / noon!

For / The

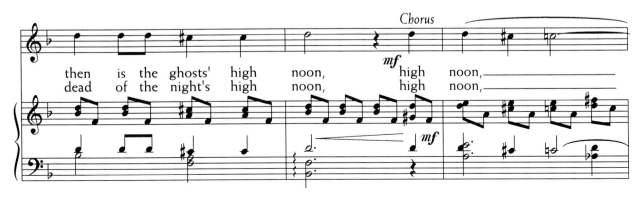

then is the ghosts' / dead of the night's

high / high

noon, / noon,

mf

high / high

noon, / noon,

mf

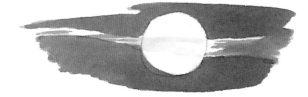

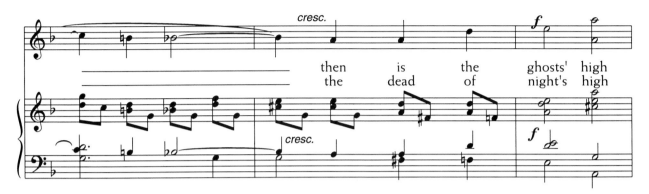

cresc.   *f*

then   is   the   ghosts' high
the   dead   of   night's high

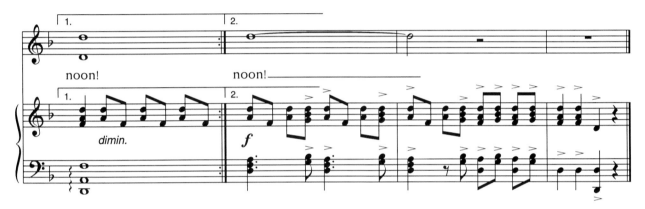

1.   2.

noon!
noon!

1.   2.

dimin.   *f*

Then One of Us Will Be a Queen

from THE GONDOLIERS

Joyously (♩ = 108)

Then one of us will be a queen, And
drive a-bout in a car-riage and pair, With the

sit on a gold-en throne, With a crown in-stead Of a
king on her left-hand side, And a milk white horse, As a

hat on her head, And di-a-monds all her own! With a
mat-ter of course, When-ev-er she wants to ride! With—

beau-ti-ful robe of gold and green, I've— al-ways un-der-
beau-ti-ful sil-ver shoes to wear Up-on— her dain-ty

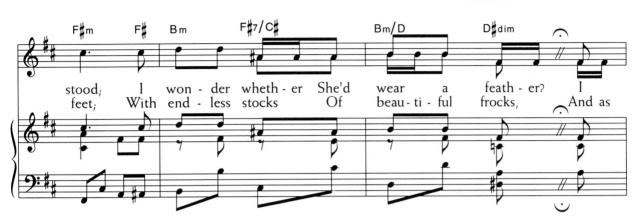

stood; I won - der wheth - er She'd wear a feath - er? I
feet; With end - less stocks Of beau - ti - ful frocks, And as

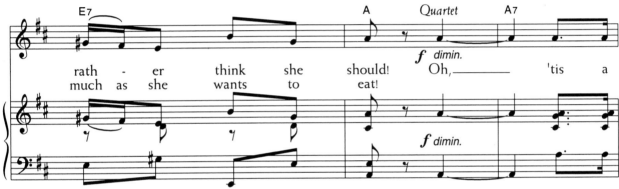

rath - er think she should! Oh,_____ 'tis a
much as she wants to eat!

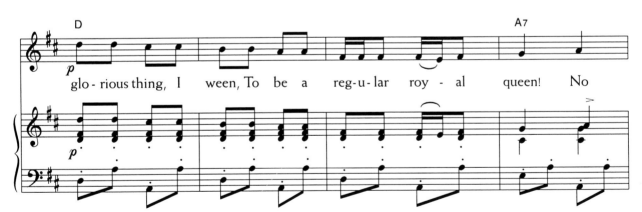

glo - rious thing, I ween, To be a reg-u-lar roy - al queen! No

half-and-half af - fair, I mean, No half - and - half__ af - fair, But a__

55

This Helmet, I Suppose

from PRINCESS IDA

Pompous but bold (♩ = 76)

This hel-met, I sup-pose, Was
tight-fit-ting cui-rass Is
things I treat the same, (I

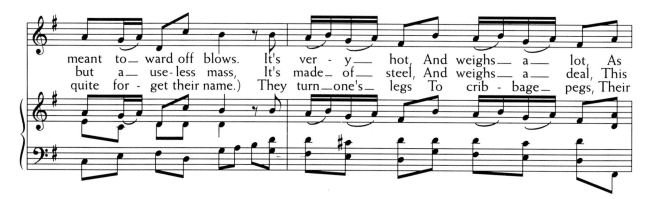

meant to — ward off blows. It's ver — y — hot, And weighs — a — lot, As
but a — use-less mass, It's made — of — steel, And weighs — a — deal, This
quite for-get their name.) They turn — one's — legs To crib-bage — pegs, Their

many a — guards-man knows, As many a guards — man knows, As
tight-fit-ting cui-rass Is but a use — less mass. A
aid I thus dis-claim, Their aid I thus dis-claim. Tho'

many a — guards-man knows, As many a — guards-man knows, So
man is — but an ass, Who fights in — a cui-rass, So
I for-get their name, Tho' I for-get their name, Their

off,_____ so off that___ hel - met goes!
off,_____ so off goes___ that cui - rass!
aid,_____ Their aid I___ thus dis - claim!

Chorus

1.   *Arac*

f Yes, yes, yes, So off that___ hel - met goes. *p* This
Yes, yes, yes, So
Yes, yes, yes, Their

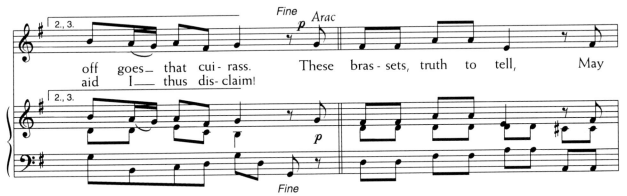

Fine *Arac*

2., 3.   *p*

off goes___ that cui - rass. These bras - sets, truth to tell, May
aid I___ thus dis - claim!

Fine

look un - com - mon well, But in a fight They're much too tight, They're

like a lob-ster—shell, ———————— They're like a lob-ster shell!

D.S. al Fine
Arac

Chorus

f Yes,   yes,   yes,   They're like a—lob-ster shell.   *p* These

D.S. al Fine

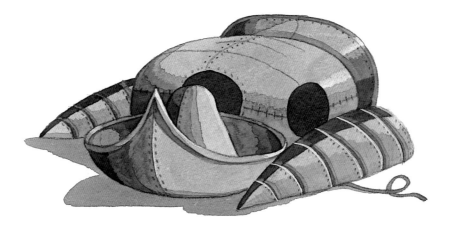

With Catlike Tread

from THE PIRATES OF PENZANCE

Strict and rhythmic (♩ = 120)

Pirates

With cat - like tread, Up - on our prey we steal; In
si - lence dread, Our cau - tious way we feel.
No sound at all! We nev - er speak a word; A
fly's foot - fall Would be dis - tinct - ly heard! Ta - ran - ta -

Police

ra, ta-ran - ta - ra! *Pirates* So steal-thi-

ly the pi -rate creeps, While all the house-hold sound-ly sleeps.

Come, friends, who plough the sea,

Truce to na - vi - ga - tion, Take an-oth - er sta - tion; Let's var - y

pi - ra - cee   With a lit -tle bur - gla - ree!   *f* Come,   friends,   who

plough   the   sea,   Truce to na - vi - ga - tion,   Take an oth - er sta - tion;

Let's   var - y   pi - ra - cee___ *ff* With a lit -tle bur – gla – ree!

I Am a Pirate King

from THE PIRATES OF PENZANCE

With a boastful swing (♩. = 80)

Pirate King

Oh,___ bet - ter far to live___ and die
When I sal - ly forth to seek___ my prey, I

Un - der the brave black flag I fly, Than play a sanc - ti -
help my - self in a roy - al way; I sink a few more

mo - nious part With a pi - rate head and a pi - rate heart!
ships,___ it's true, Than a well - bred mon - arch ought to do!

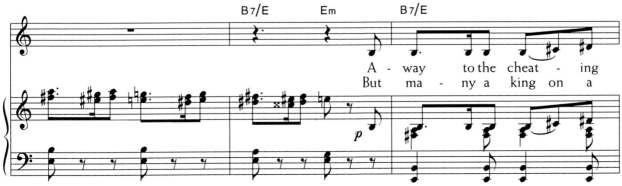

A - way to the cheat - ing
But ma - ny a king on a

world go you,
first - class throne,

Where
If he

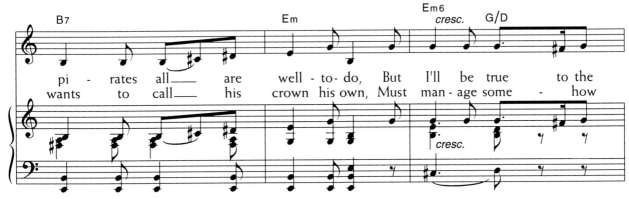

pi - rates all__ are well - to - do, But I'll be true to the
wants to call__ his crown his own, Must man - age some - how

song I sing, And live__ and die a pi - rate king, For__ I
to get through More dir - ty work than ever I do, Though__ I

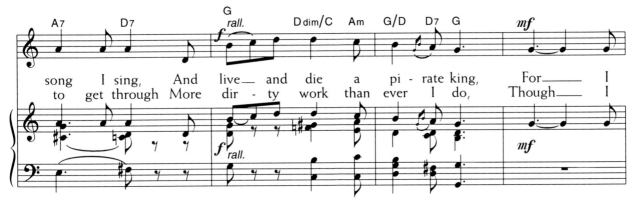

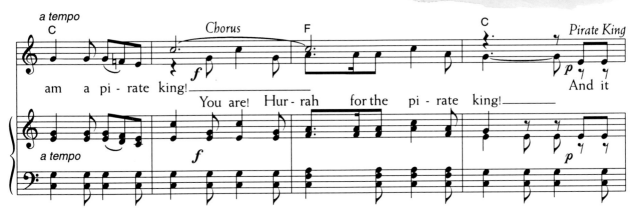

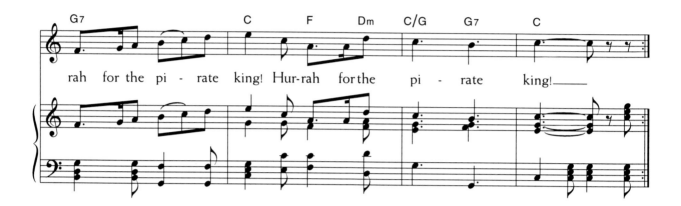

rah for the pi - rate king! Hur-rah for the pi - rate king!____

A Magnet Hung in a Hardware Shop

from PATIENCE

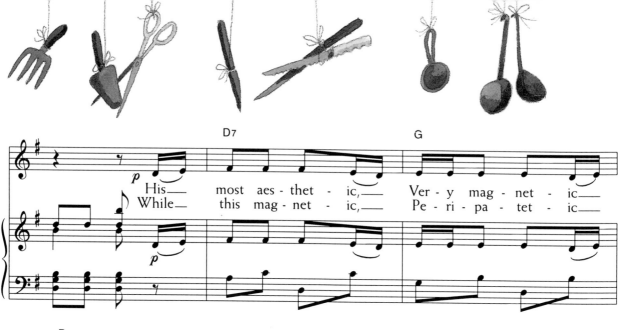

Chorus of Maidens

I can whee-dle A knife or a nee-dle, Why not a sil-ver churn?"
no en-deav-or Can mag-net ev-er At-tract a sil-ver churn!

Ex-Library: Friends of
Lake County Public Library

Index of Song Titles